THE SECRET SOCIETY OF MONSTER HUNTERS

THE STOLEN KRAKEN

by Kate Tremaine

illustrated by Jared Sams

Published in the United States of America by Cherry Lake Publishing Group
Ann Arbor, Michigan
www.cherrylakepublishing.com

Reading Adviser: Marla Conn, MS, Ed., Literacy specialist, Read-Ability, Inc.

Book Design: Book Buddy Media

Photo Credits: page 1: ©sanchesnet1/iStock / Getty Images ; page 5: ©Fred Palumbo/New York World-Telegram & Sun Collection/Library of Congress / Wikimedia ; page 9: ©bobbieo/E+ / Getty Images ; page 13: ©Serhii Yakovliev/ iStock / Getty Images ; page 25: ©Xarlyxa/iStock / Getty Images ; page 30: ©miflippo/iStock / Getty Images ; background: ©Lisa Norris Artworks/iStock / Getty Images ; background: ©OpenClipart-Vectors / Pixabay(facts); background: ©MarjanNo / Pixabay(lined paper) ; background: ©BreathlessDesign / Pixabay(sidebars)

Torch Graphic Press is an imprint of Cherry Lake Publishing Group.

Library of Congress Cataloging-in-Publication Data has been filed and is available at catalog.loc.gov

Cherry Lake Publishing Group would like to acknowledge the work of the Partnership for 21st Century Learning, a Network of Battelle for Kids. Please visit http://www.battelleforkids.org/networks/p21 for more information.

Printed in the United States of America
Corporate Graphics

TABLE OF CONTENTS

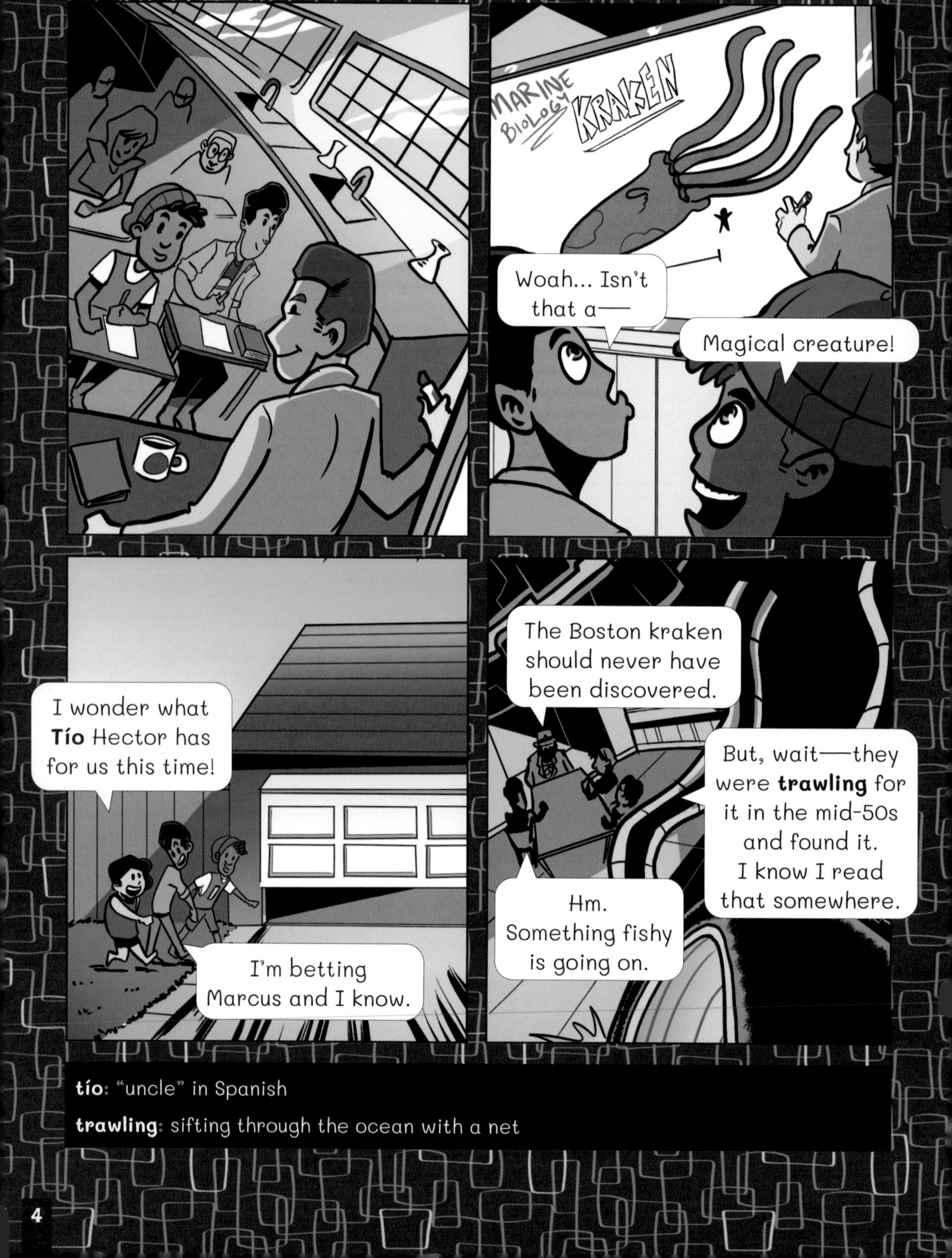
MARINE BIOLOGY
KRAKEN
Woah... Isn't that a—
Magical creature!
I wonder what **Tío** Hector has for us this time!
I'm betting Marcus and I know.
The Boston kraken should never have been discovered.
But, wait—they were **trawling** for it in the mid-50s and found it. I know I read that somewhere.
Hm. Something fishy is going on.

tío: "uncle" in Spanish

trawling: sifting through the ocean with a net

TIPS FOR THE DECADE

The 1950s are often known as a **conformist** decade. Pop culture, like TV and music, focused on traditional male and female roles. But women and other groups had gained new and more powerful places in society during World War II. These groups began to push back.

* **Feminism** and **civil rights** got a new start in the 1950s.

* Betty Friedan and Dr. Martin Luther King Jr. spoke out against racism and sexism.

* The Montgomery Bus Boycott was a protest against **segregation**. African Americans no longer wanted to be forced to sit in the back of the bus. They stopped taking the bus for a year.

* Television use was rising after the invention of color TV. There were only four TV channels.

conformist: accepting of social norms and the established culture

feminism: the belief that men and women are equal

civil rights: the rights for people to have freedom and equality

segregation: the separation of people based on the color of their skin

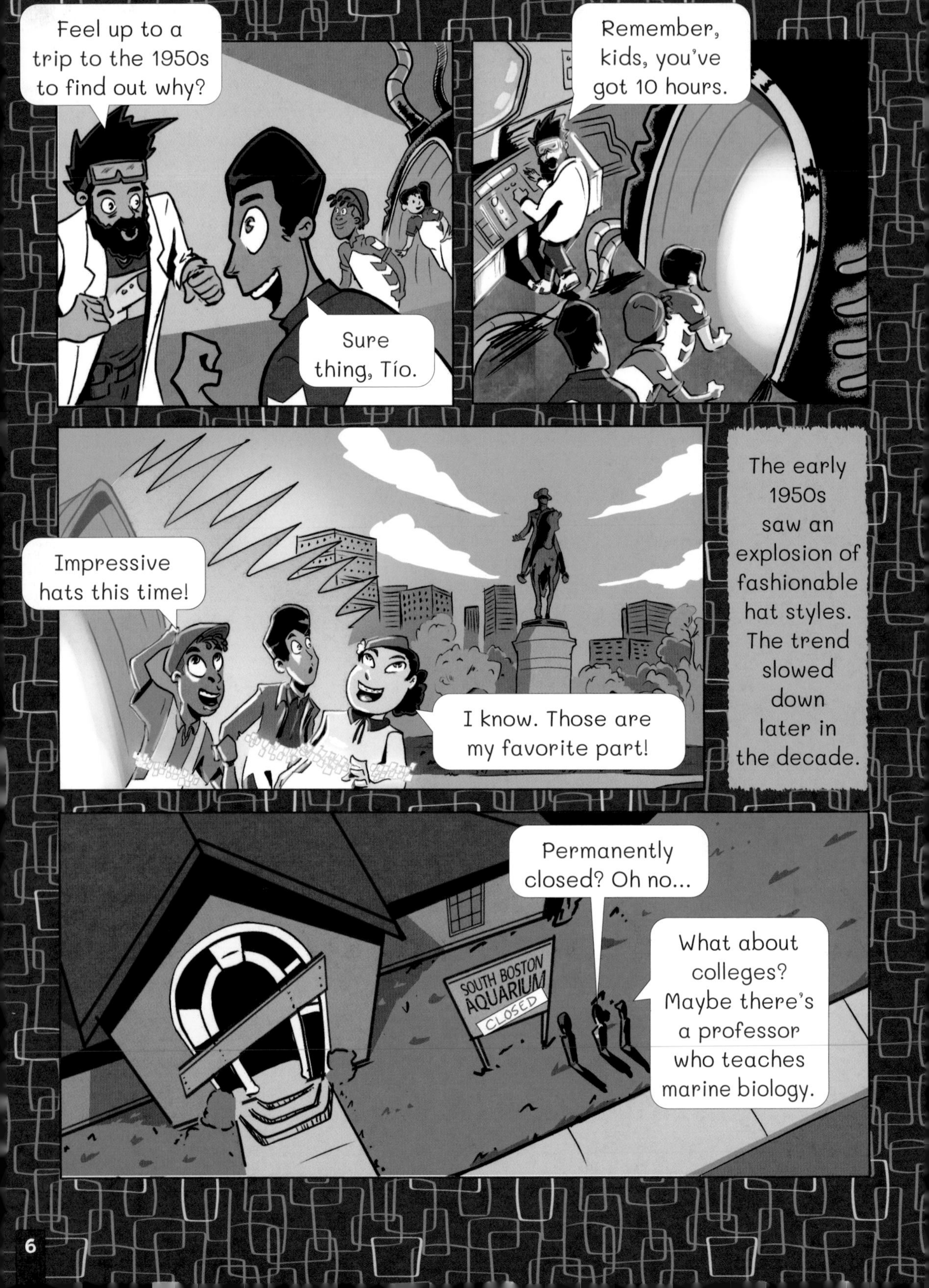
Feel up to a trip to the 1950s to find out why?
Sure thing, Tío.
Remember, kids, you've got 10 hours.
Impressive hats this time!
I know. Those are my favorite part!
The early 1950s saw an explosion of fashionable hat styles. The trend slowed down later in the decade.
Permanently closed? Oh no...
What about colleges? Maybe there's a professor who teaches marine biology.
SOUTH BOSTON AQUARIUM
CLOSED

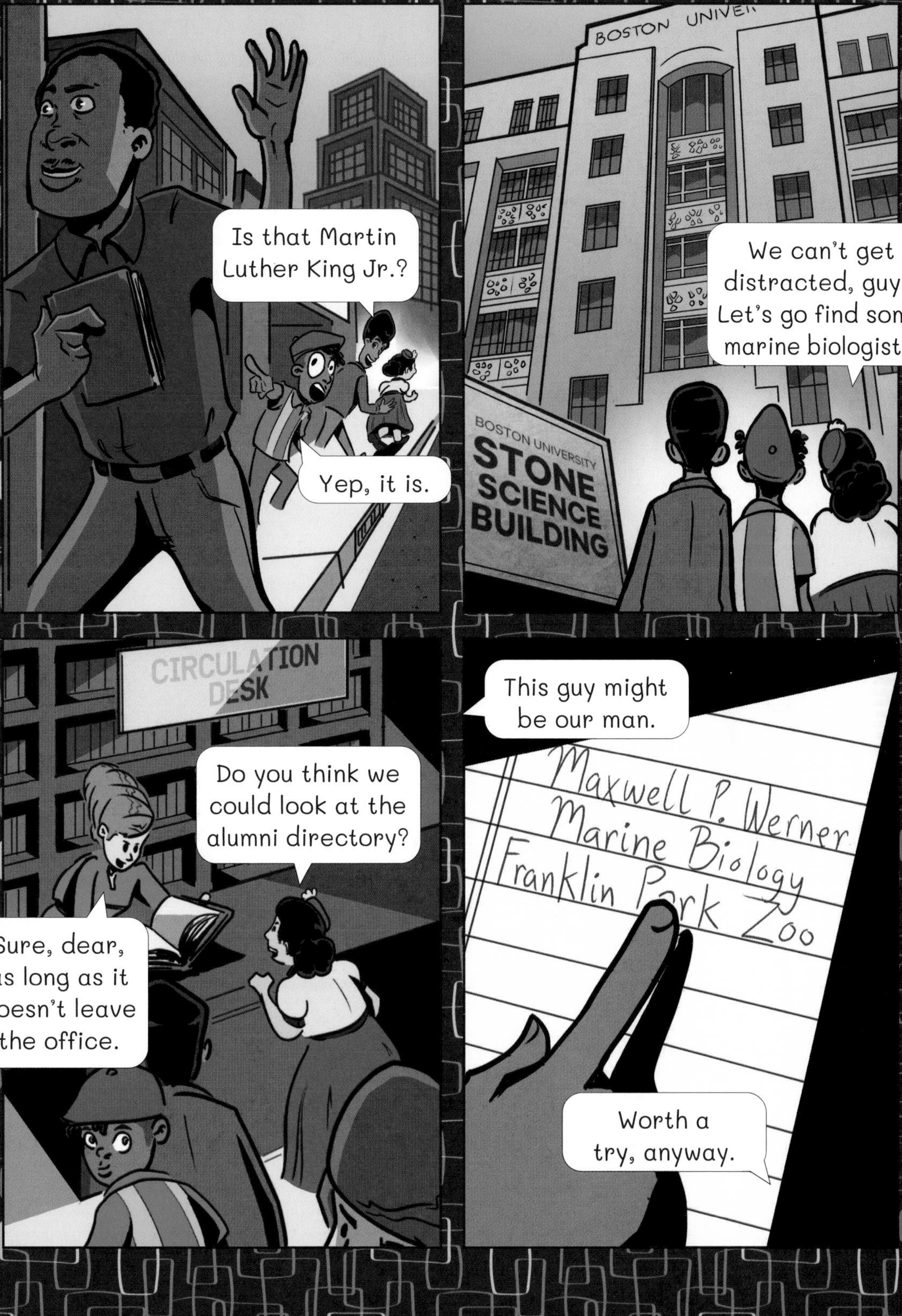
Is that Martin Luther King Jr.?
Yep, it is.
BOSTON UNIVER
BOSTON UNIVERSITY STONE SCIENCE BUILDING
We can't get distracted, guys! Let's go find some marine biologists!
CIRCULATION DESK
Do you think we could look at the alumni directory?
Sure, dear, as long as it doesn't leave the office.
This guy might be our man.
Maxwell P. Werner
Marine Biology
Franklin Park Zoo
Worth a try, anyway.

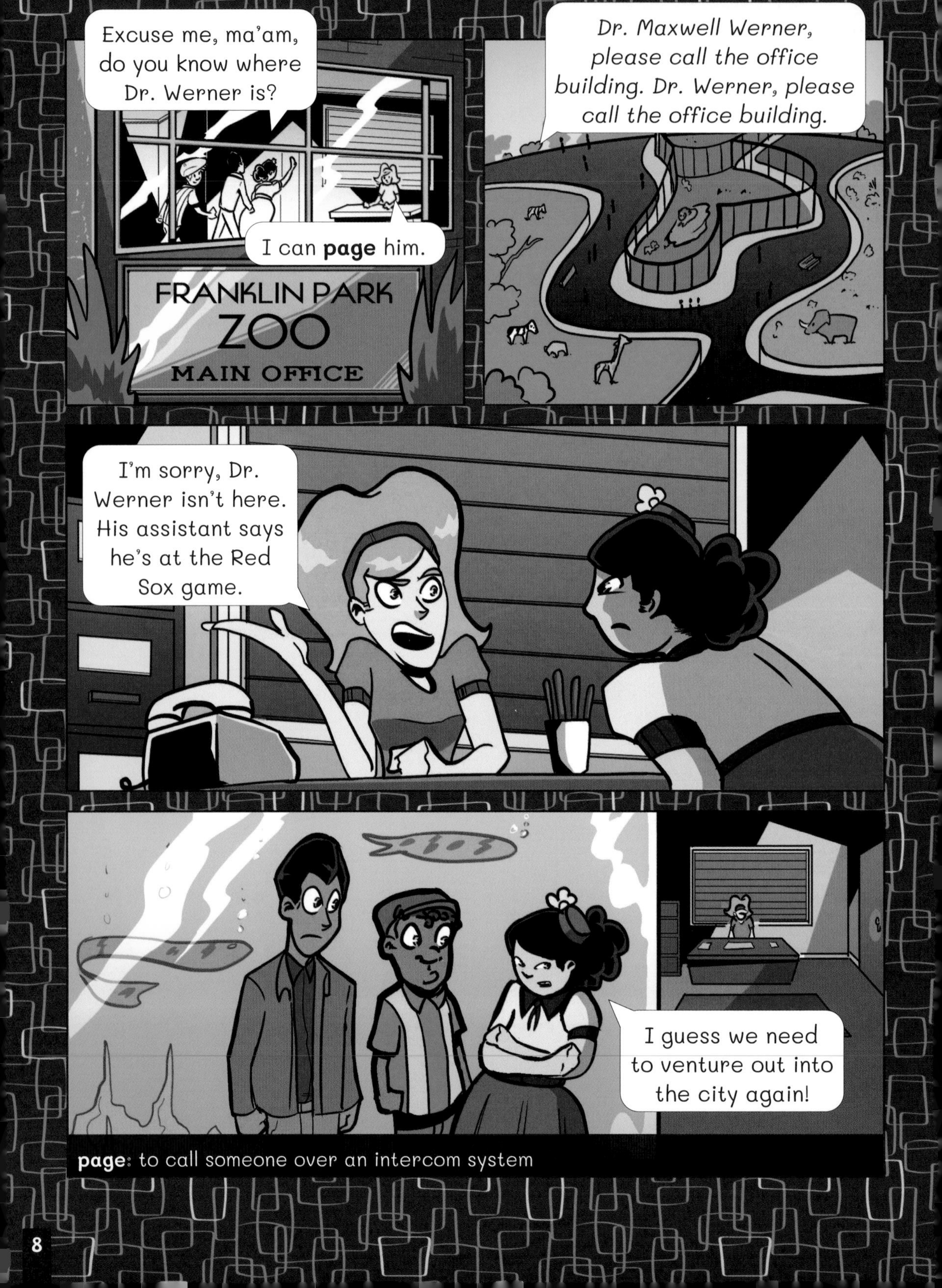
Excuse me, ma'am, do you know where Dr. Werner is?
I can **page** him.
FRANKLIN PARK ZOO MAIN OFFICE
Dr. Maxwell Werner, please call the office building. Dr. Werner, please call the office building.
I'm sorry, Dr. Werner isn't here. His assistant says he's at the Red Sox game.
I guess we need to venture out into the city again!

page: to call someone over an intercom system

PACKING LIST

During World War II, cloth was **rationed**. When this rationing ended, women began wearing more glamorous clothing.

Women's fashion included:

* Narrow waists and wide, full skirts

* Shirts with decorative collars

* Bright colors and patterns

* Accessories like hats, purses, and gloves (even in the summer!)

* Poodle skirts, bobby sox, and saddle shoes for girls

Men's fashion included:

* Suits in dark colors, with ties and pocket squares

* Wingtip shoes

* Thick cardigans, including the letter sweaters popular in high school

* Accessories like hats and different types of shoes, from wingtip to penny loafers to blue suede

rationed: when each person is allowed only a certain amount of something

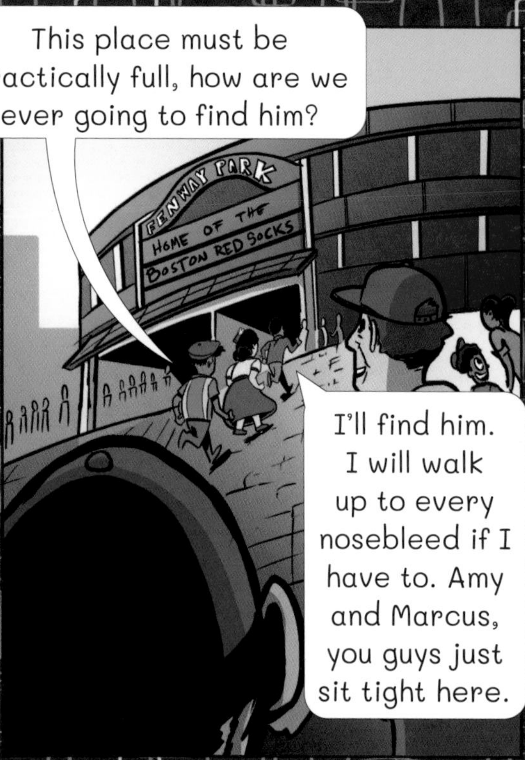
This place must be practically full, how are we ever going to find him?
FENWAY PARK
HOME OF THE BOSTON RED SOCKS
I'll find him. I will walk up to every nosebleed if I have to. Amy and Marcus, you guys just sit tight here.

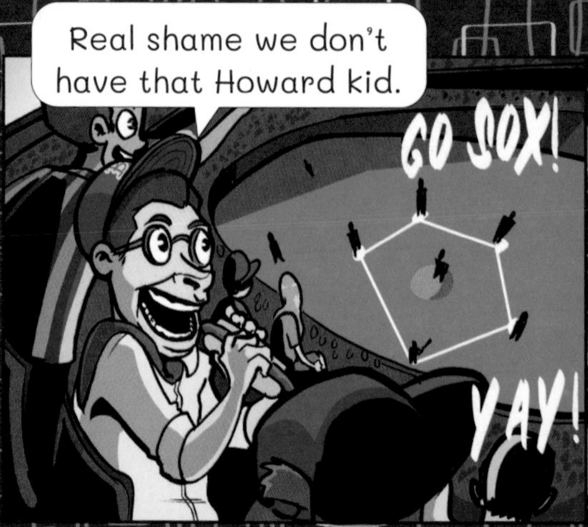
Real shame we don't have that Howard kid.
GO SOX!
YAY!

In the 1950s, baseball was the most popular sport in the United States. In 1947, Jackie Robinson had broken the "color barrier" of segregation in baseball, and by the end of the 50s, every major league team had **integrated**.

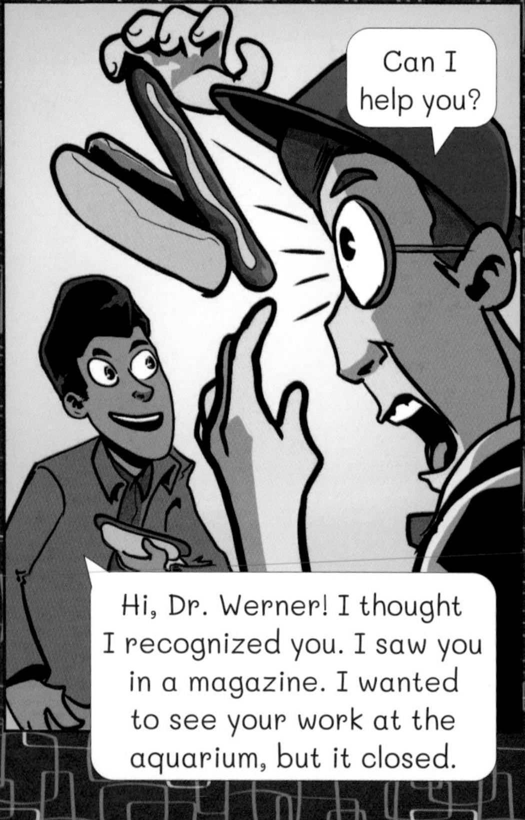
Can I help you?
Hi, Dr. Werner! I thought I recognized you. I saw you in a magazine. I wanted to see your work at the aquarium, but it closed.

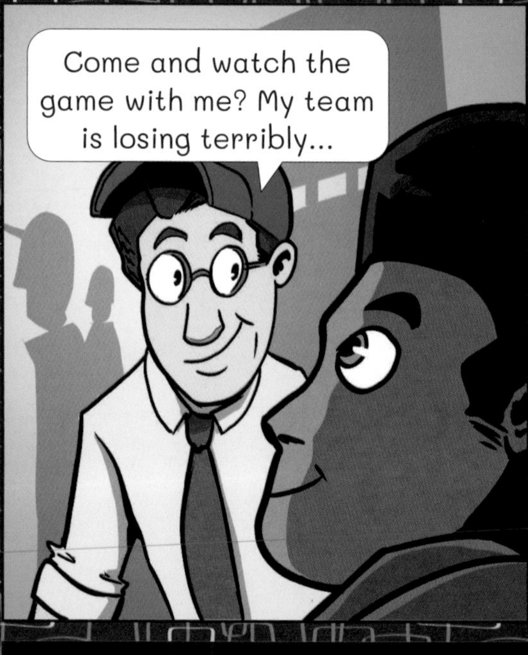
Come and watch the game with me? My team is losing terribly...

integrated: united people of different races in the same group or institution

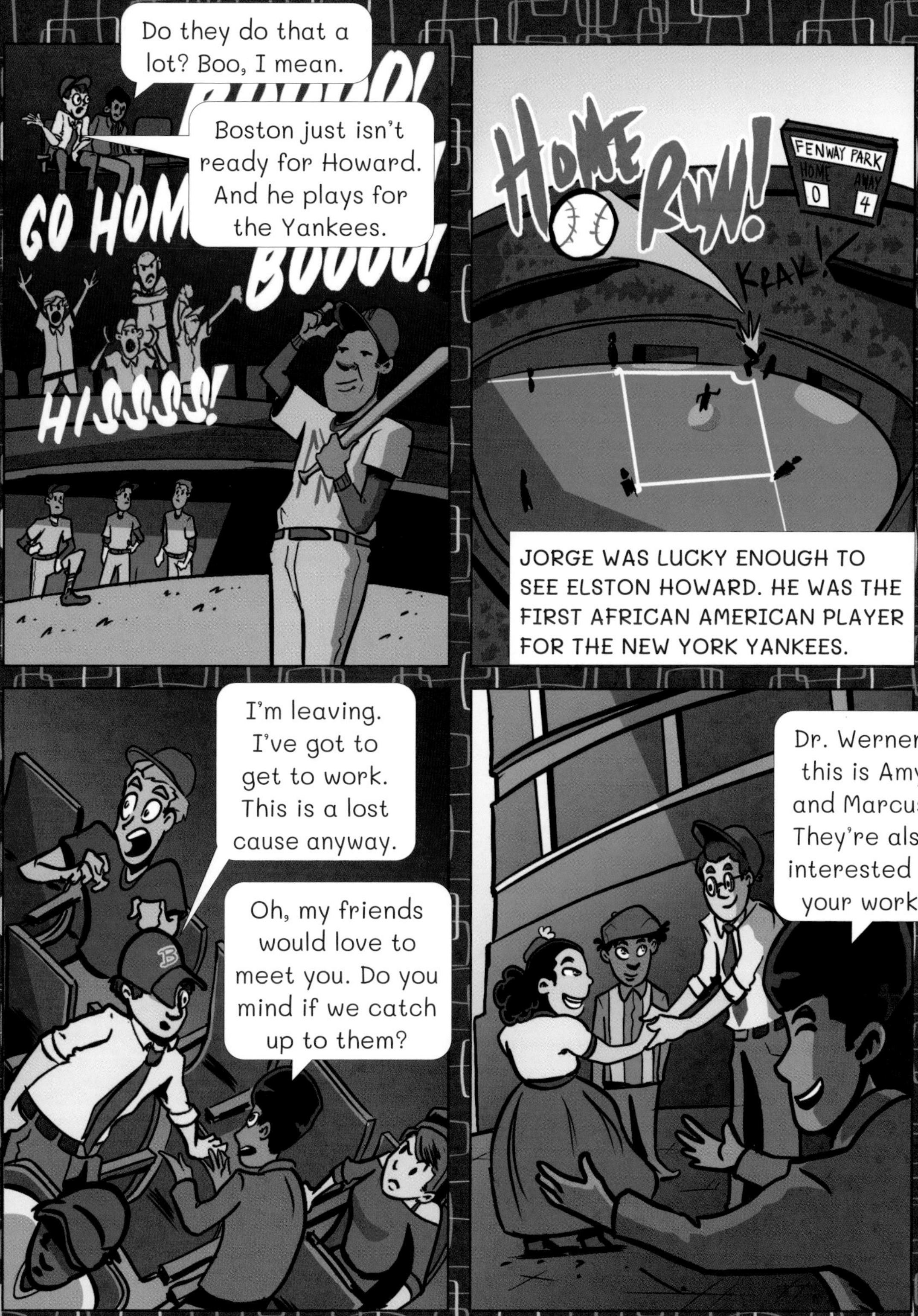
Do they do that a lot? Boo, I mean.
Boston just isn't ready for Howard. And he plays for the Yankees.
HISSSS!
HOME RUN!
FENWAY PARK
HOME AWAY
0 4
KRAK!
JORGE WAS LUCKY ENOUGH TO SEE ELSTON HOWARD. HE WAS THE FIRST AFRICAN AMERICAN PLAYER FOR THE NEW YORK YANKEES.
I'm leaving. I've got to get to work. This is a lost cause anyway.
Oh, my friends would love to meet you. Do you mind if we catch up to them?
Dr. Werner, this is Amy and Marcus. They're also interested in your work.

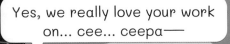

Yes, we really love your work on... cee... ceepa—

Cephalopods!

Really? Has my work made it into universities?

Oh, yes, sir. Our biology teacher—uh, professor—taught us all about your new identification method. We'd love to see it in the field.

Oh, I—I'd love that. I have been waiting for someone to take it seriously! I'm going out on the harbor in a few hours!

Fantastic! We would love to come.

See you in a bit!

I guess we'd better change into our kraken-finding clothes!

cephalopods: a group of sea animals with tentacles, like octopus and squid

WHAT IS THE KRAKEN?

The kraken is the largest monster in the sea. This half-squid, half-crab has a sharp beak and many rows of huge teeth. Each of its 12 **tentacles** ends in a huge claw. The tentacles also have hundreds of spiked suction cups on them. What else is known about the kraken?

* The kraken lives in the caves of deep northern oceans.

* It crawls along the **ocean floor**.

* It lures animals by vomiting bait. Animals move into its mouth, thinking they have found food.

* The kraken is more than just large and strong. It leaves behind black oil that blinds its prey, and its spit is poison.

* The kraken can regrow its tentacles if they are damaged.

* Magic doesn't affect the kraken. And because it's so huge and powerful, it's very hard to stop.

Remember, we need to get him talking about the kraken.

And we need to keep an eye out for it too!

Arthropods aren't my specialty, but they're part of my work for the zoo. But hopefully we'll find some cephalopods too.

I'm sure you can teach us a lot about arthropods *and* cephalopods.

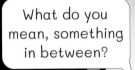

Maybe something... in between?

What do you mean, something in between?

arthropods: invertebrate animals with a hard shell, like insects, crabs, and spiders

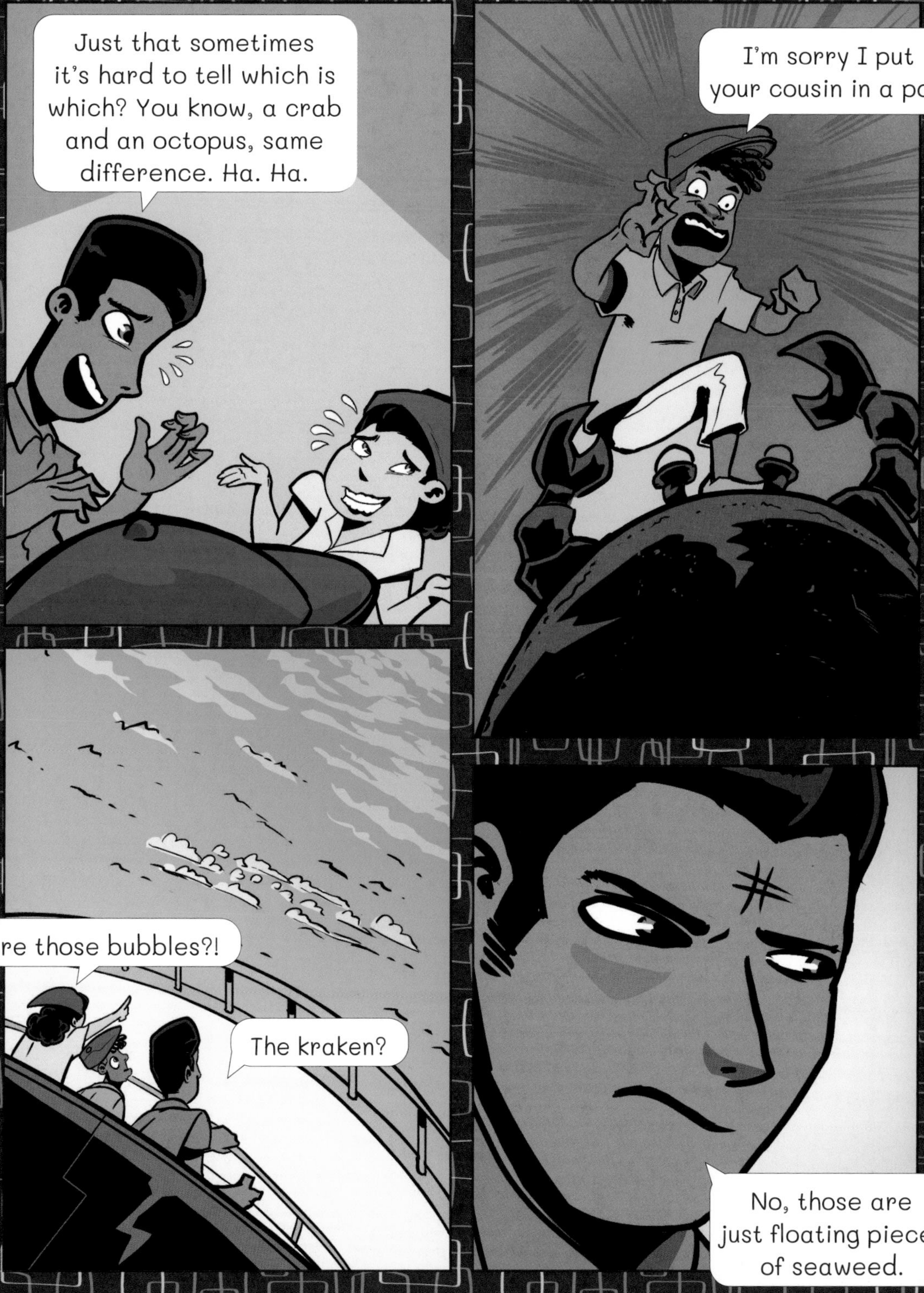
Just that sometimes it's hard to tell which is which? You know, a crab and an octopus, same difference. Ha. Ha.
I'm sorry I put your cousin in a pot!
Are those bubbles?!
The kraken?
No, those are just floating pieces of seaweed.

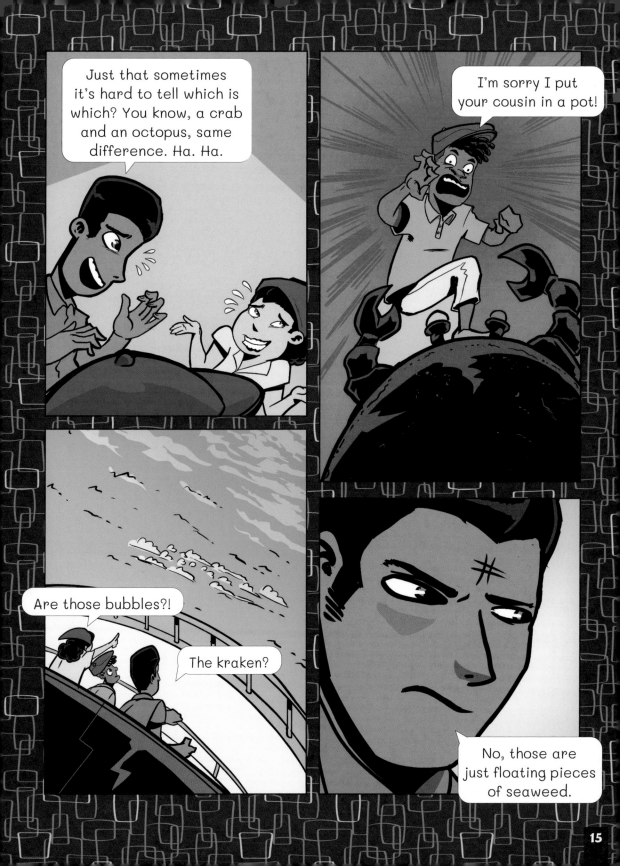

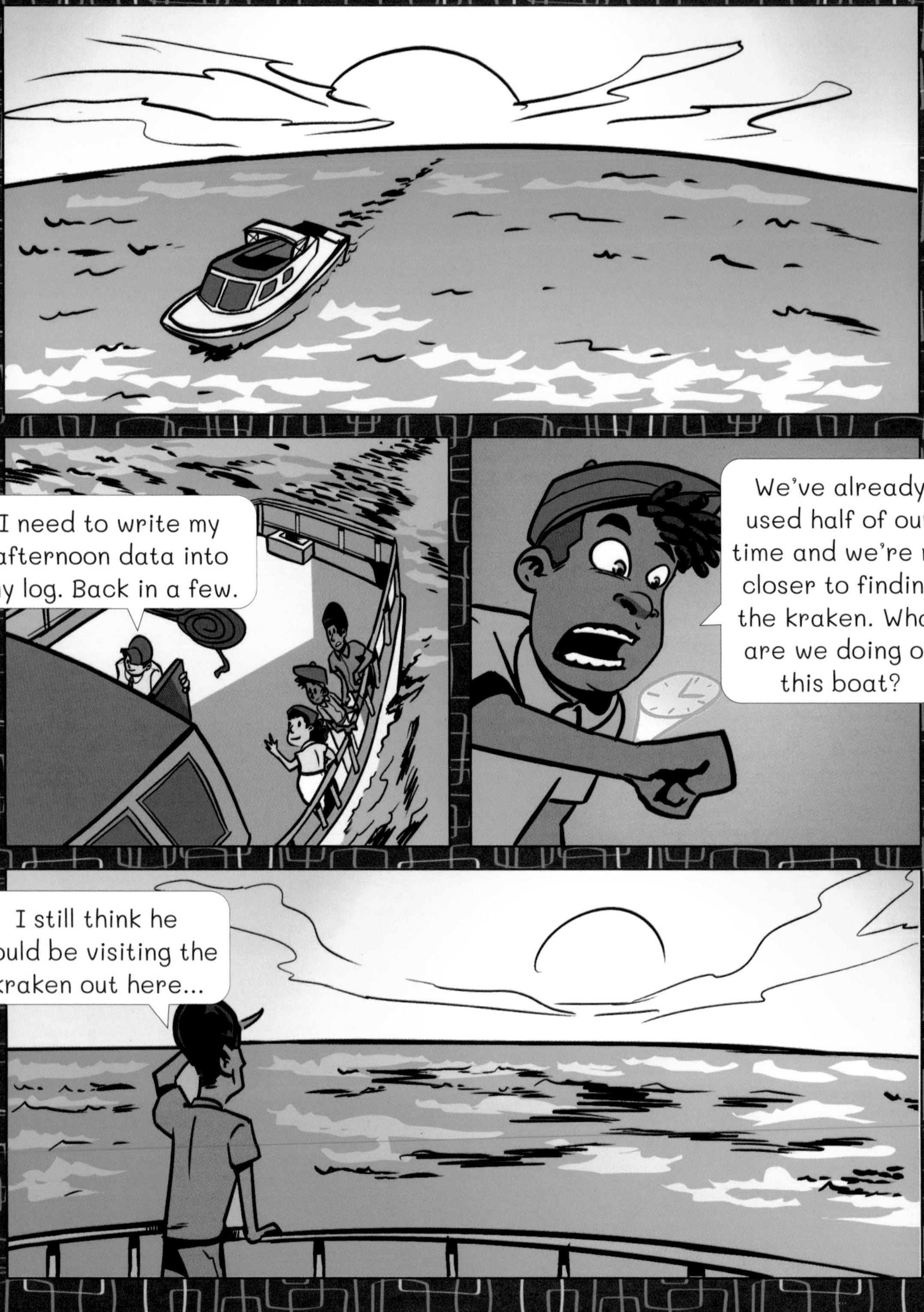
I need to write my afternoon data into my log. Back in a few.
We've already used half of our time and we're no closer to finding the kraken. What are we doing on this boat?
I still think he could be visiting the kraken out here...

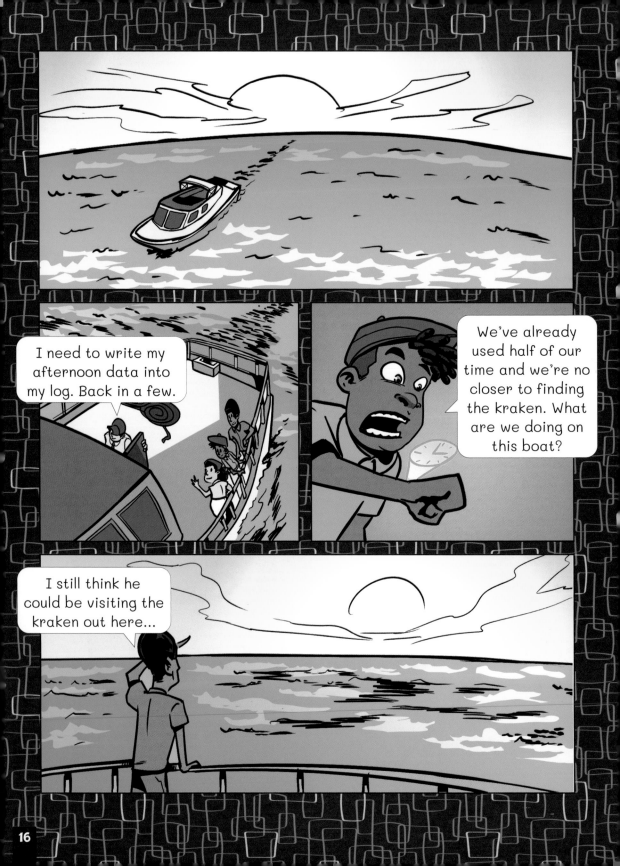

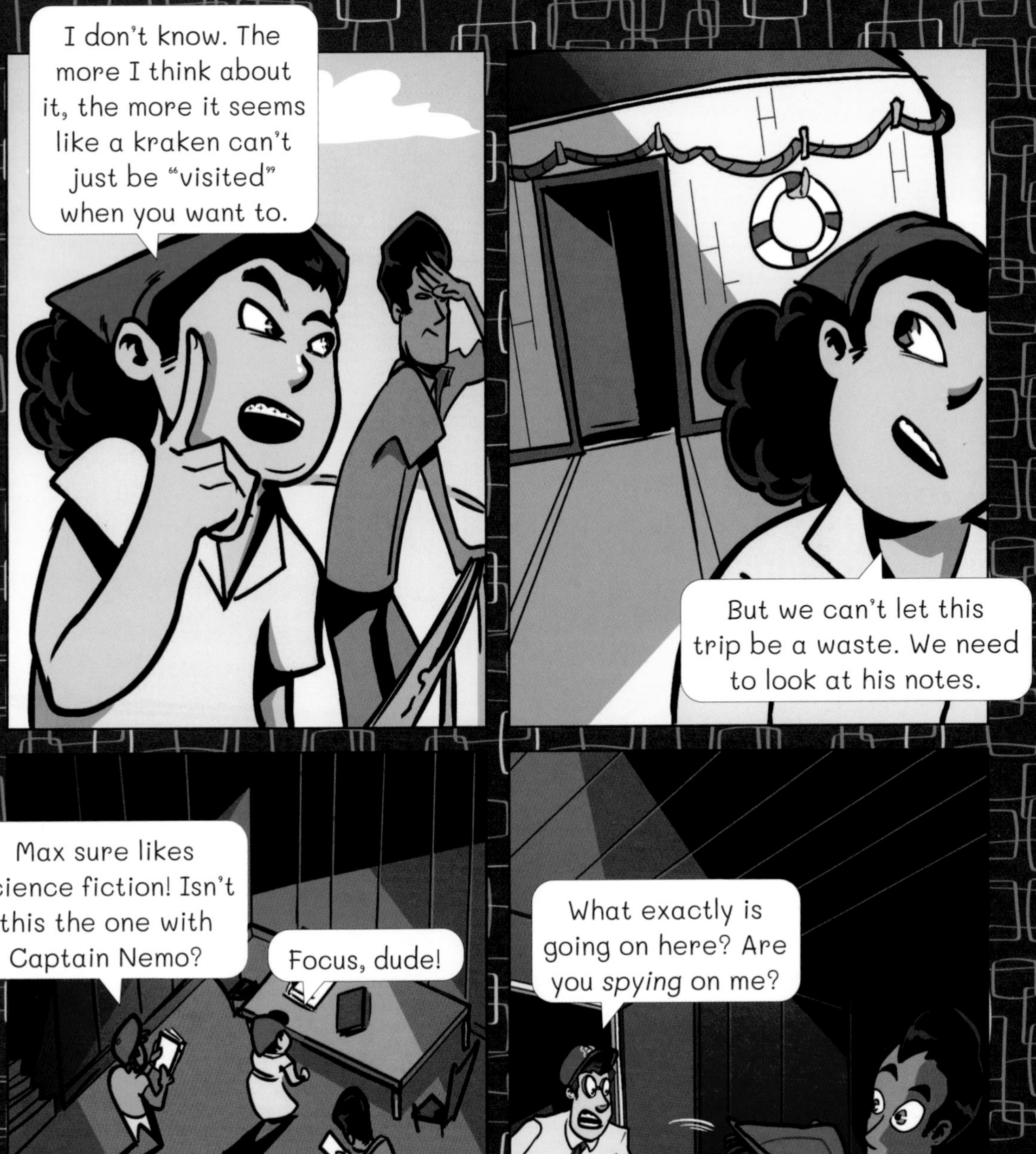
I don't know. The more I think about it, the more it seems like a kraken can't just be "visited" when you want to.
But we can't let this trip be a waste. We need to look at his notes.
Max sure likes science fiction! Isn't this the one with Captain Nemo?
Focus, dude!
Science fiction became popular in the 1950s. New technology created during WWII inspired many ideas. Science fiction magazines and novels became very popular.
What exactly is going on here? Are you *spying* on me?
We're just, um, interested... Marcus is a huge fan of cephalopods.

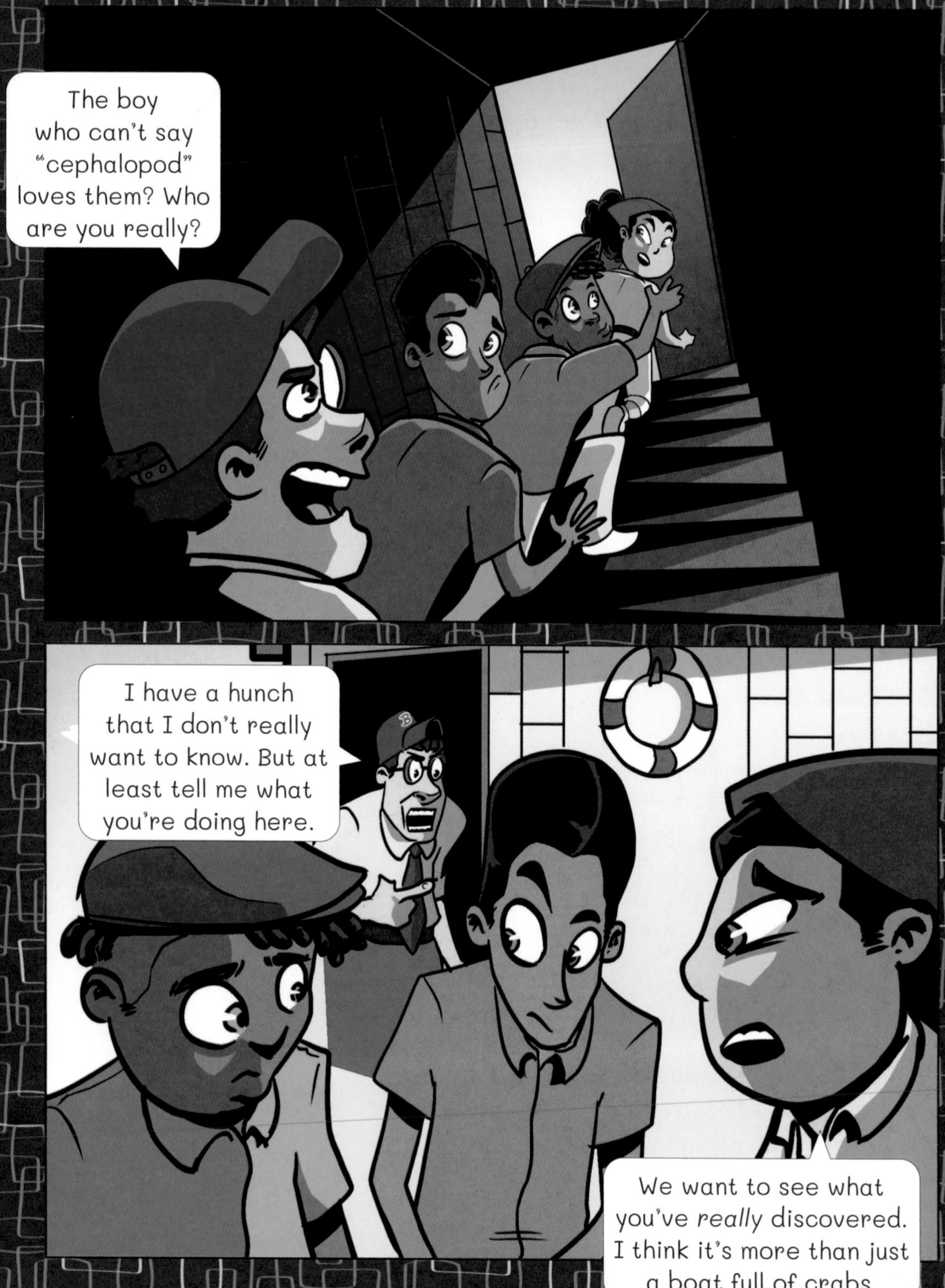
The boy who can't say "cephalopod" loves them? Who are you really?
I have a hunch that I don't really want to know. But at least tell me what you're doing here.
We want to see what you've *really* discovered. I think it's more than just a boat full of crabs.

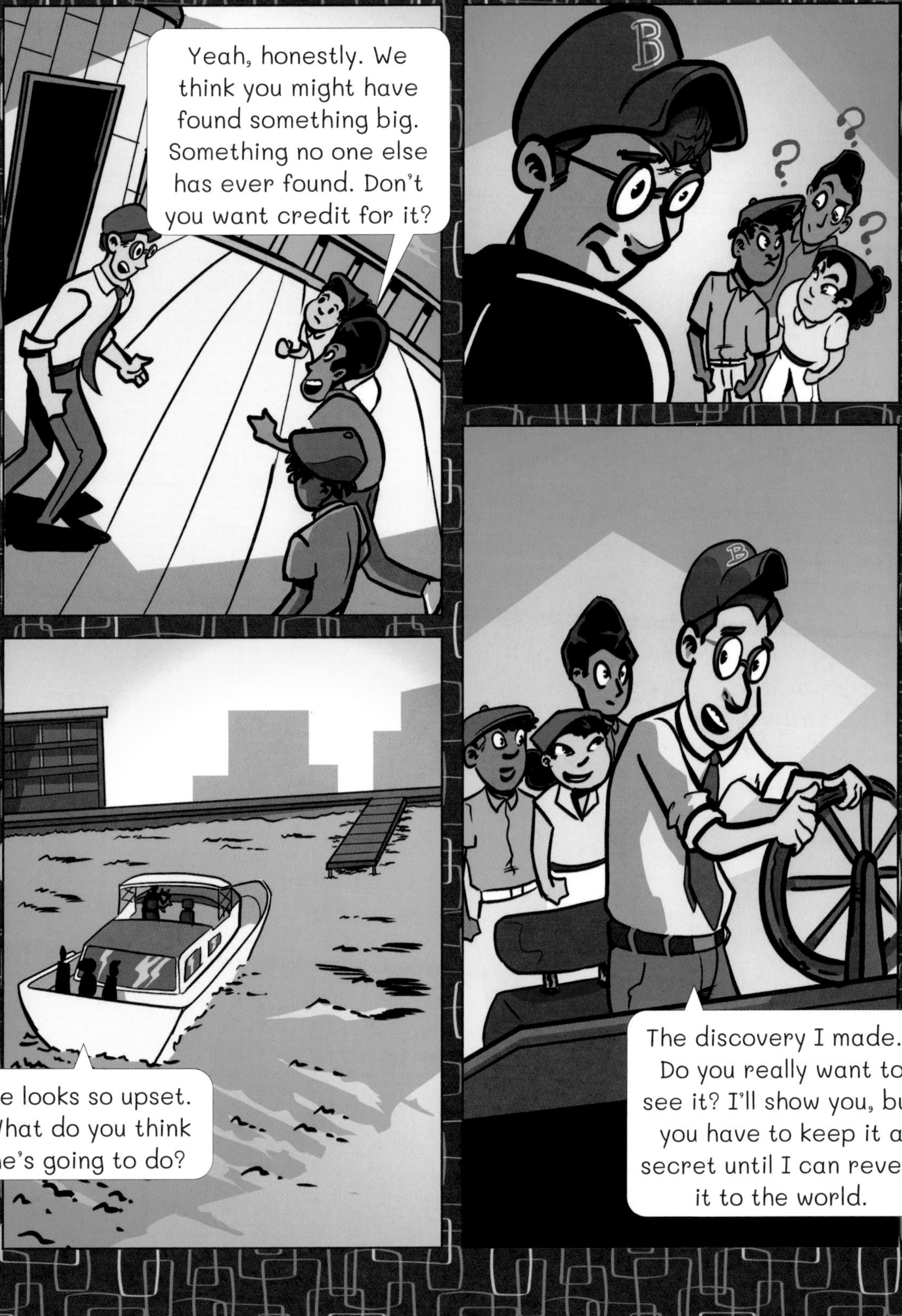
Yeah, honestly. We think you might have found something big. Something no one else has ever found. Don't you want credit for it?
?
?
?
The discovery I made... Do you really want to see it? I'll show you, but you have to keep it a secret until I can reveal it to the world.
He looks so upset. What do you think he's going to do?

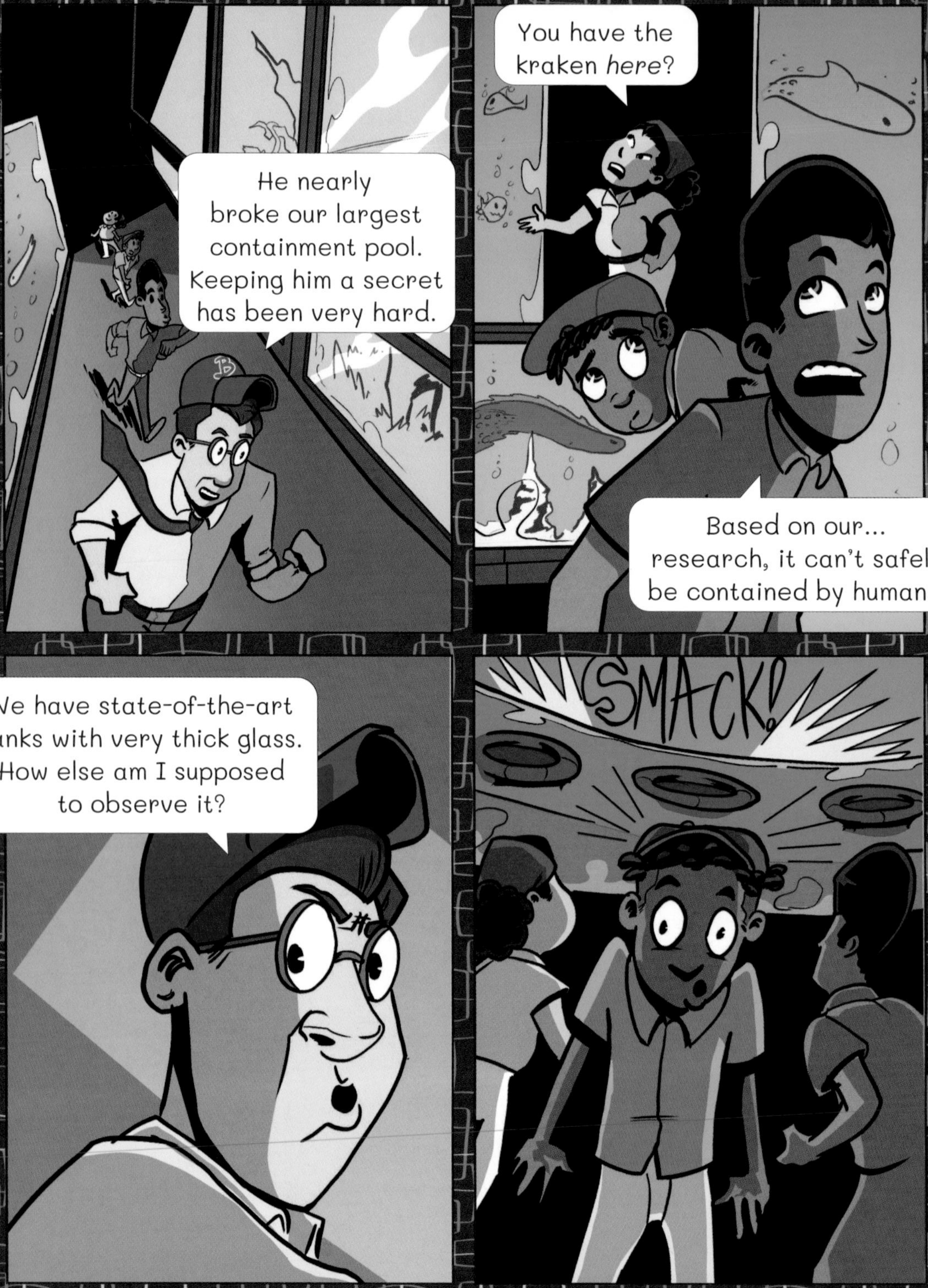
He nearly broke our largest containment pool. Keeping him a secret has been very hard.
You have the kraken *here*?
Based on our... research, it can't safely be contained by humans.
We have state-of-the-art tanks with very thick glass. How else am I supposed to observe it?
SMACK!

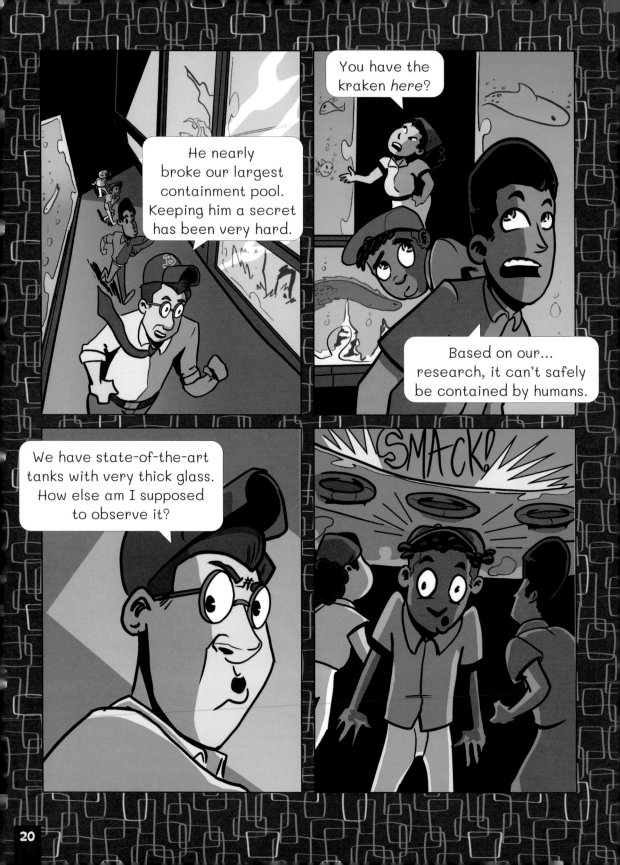

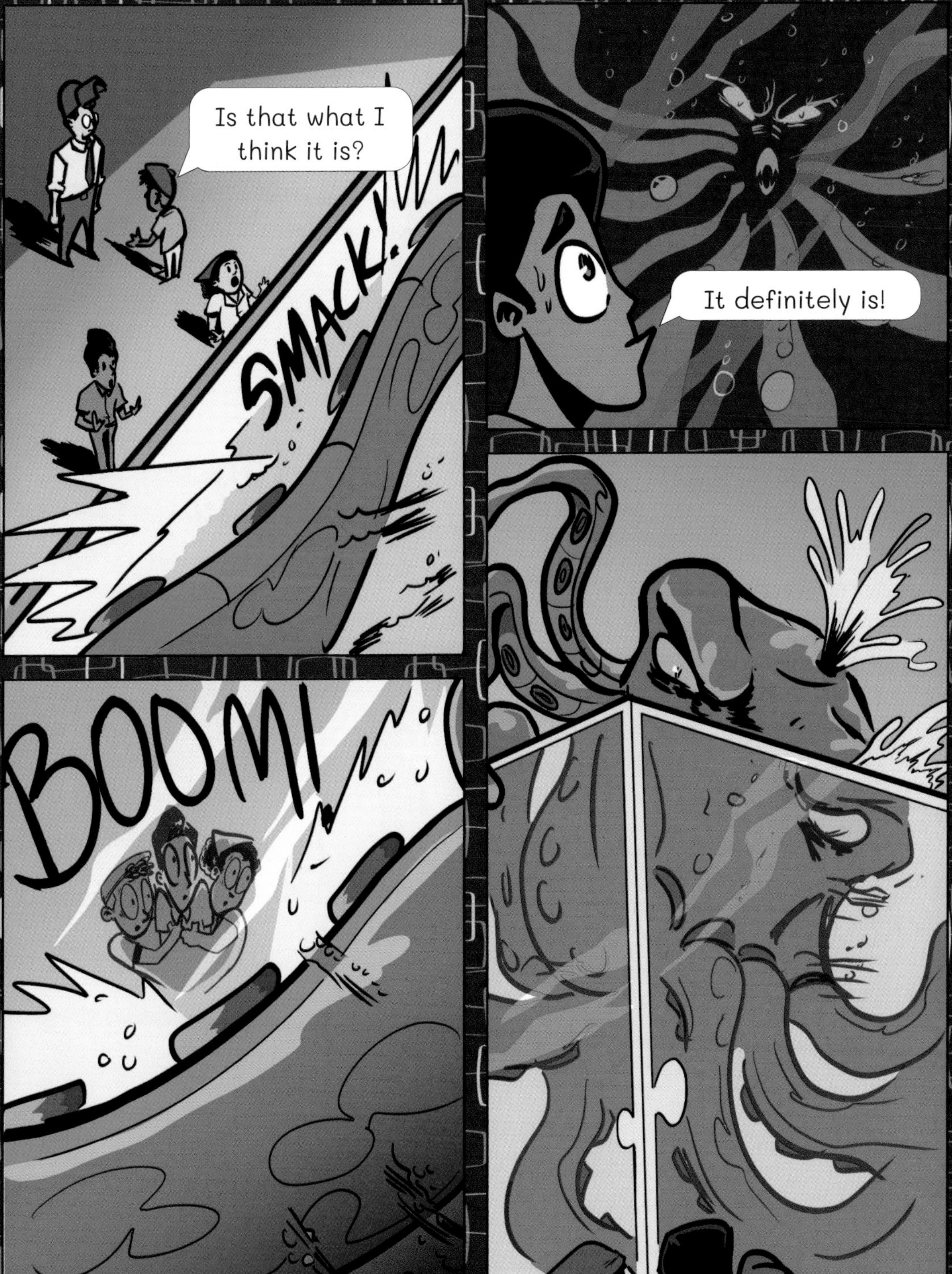

Is that what I think it is?
SMACK!
It definitely is!
BOOM!

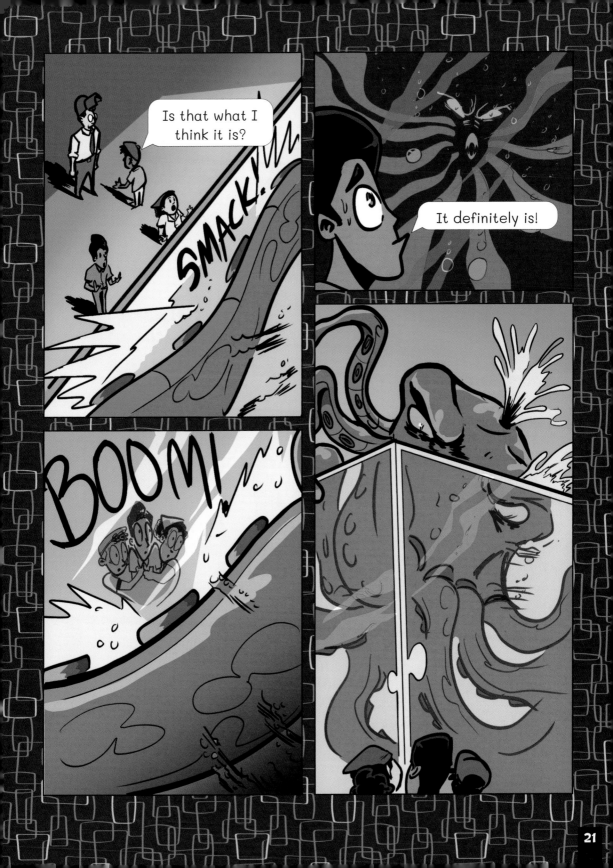

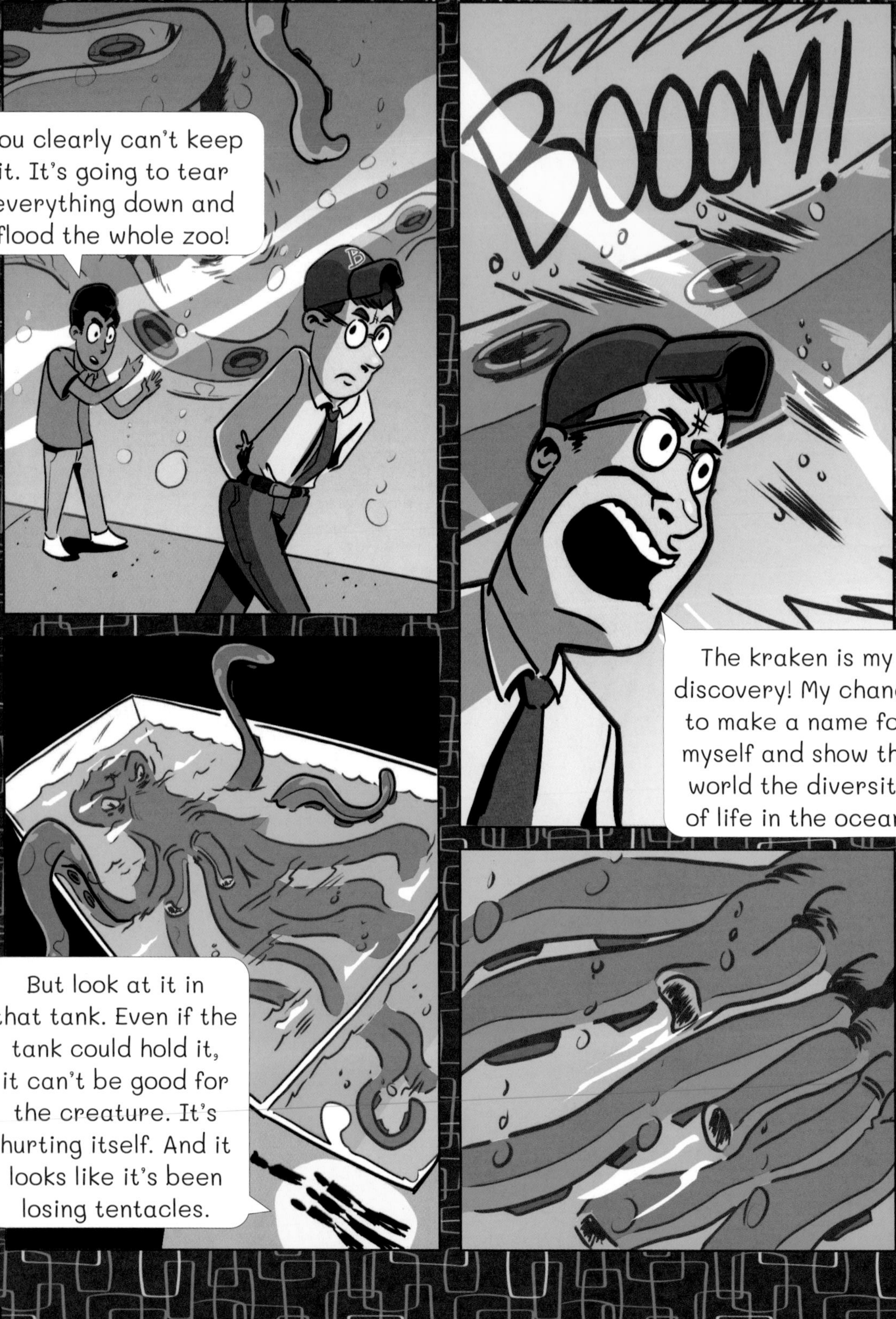
You clearly can't keep it. It's going to tear everything down and flood the whole zoo!
BOOOM!
The kraken is my discovery! My chance to make a name for myself and show the world the diversity of life in the ocean!
But look at it in that tank. Even if the tank could hold it, it can't be good for the creature. It's hurting itself. And it looks like it's been losing tentacles.

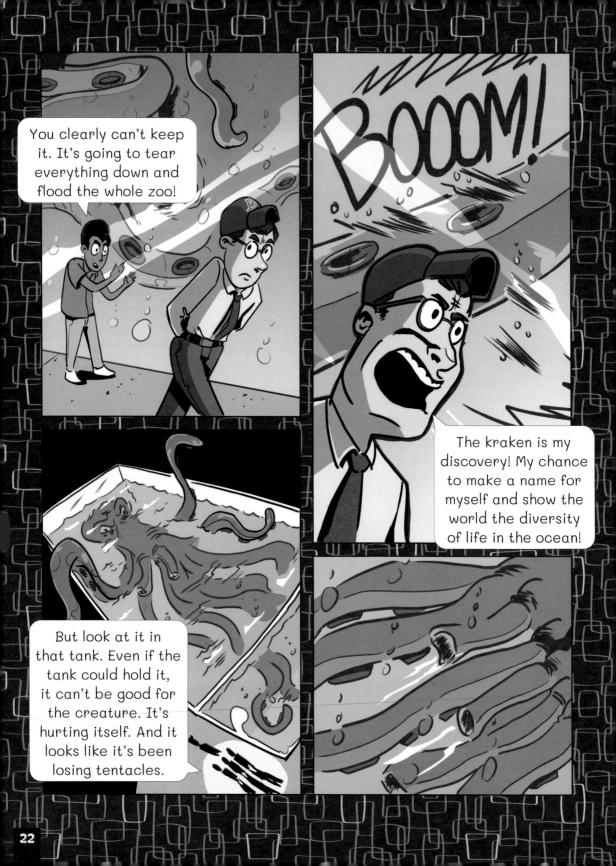

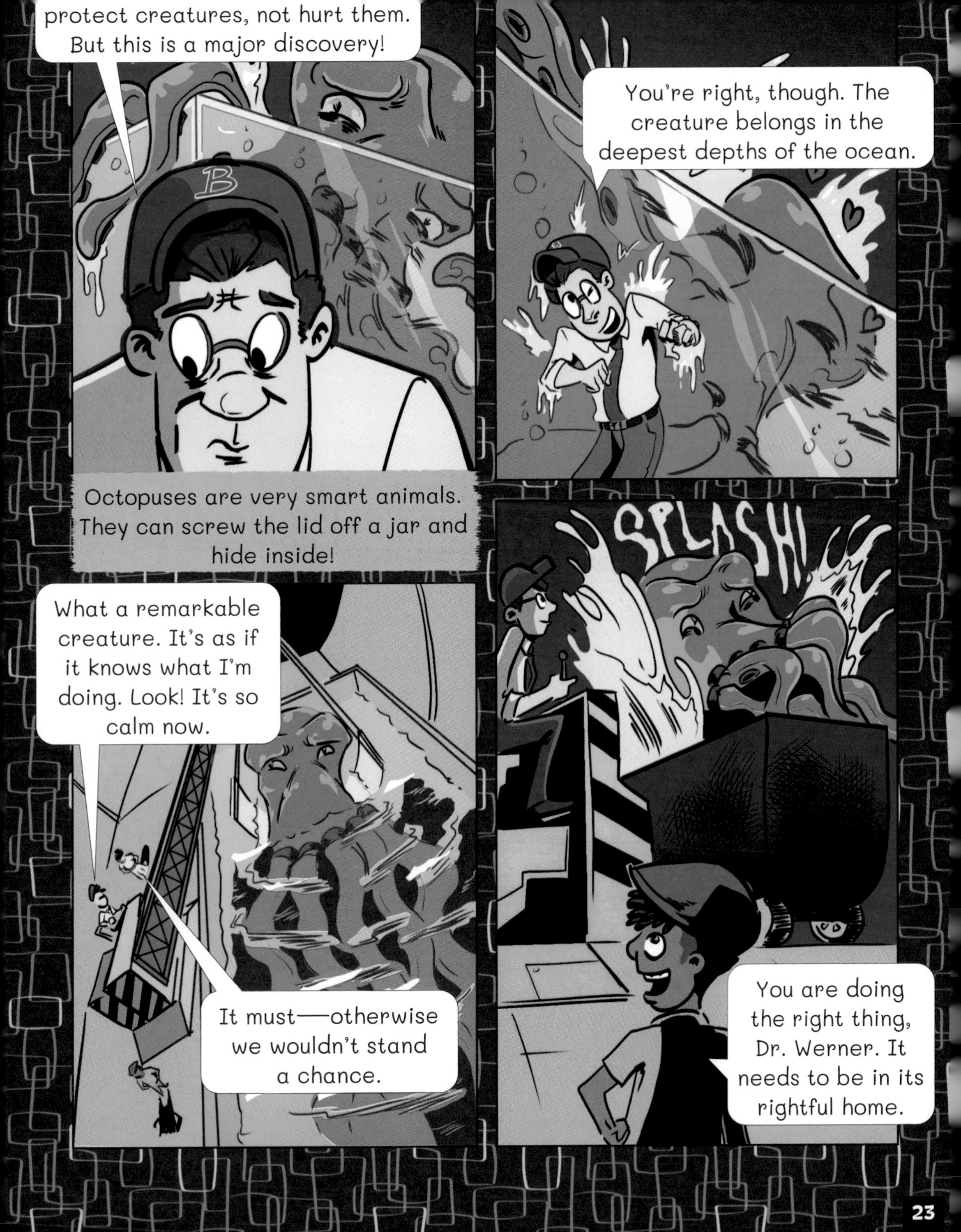
protect creatures, not hurt them. But this is a major discovery!
You're right, though. The creature belongs in the deepest depths of the ocean.
Octopuses are very smart animals. They can screw the lid off a jar and hide inside!
What a remarkable creature. It's as if it knows what I'm doing. Look! It's so calm now.
It must—otherwise we wouldn't stand a chance.
SPLASH!
You are doing the right thing, Dr. Werner. It needs to be in its rightful home.

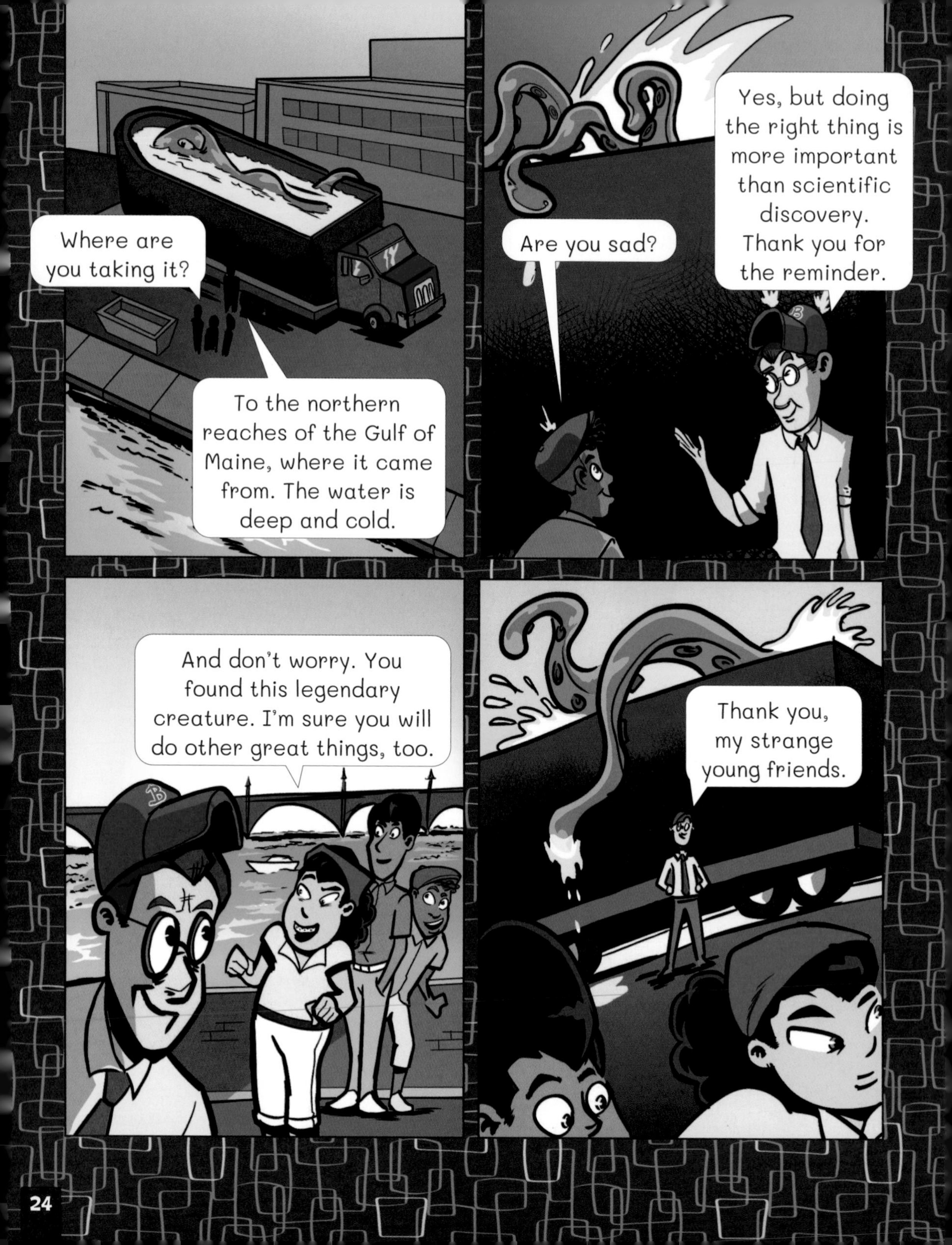

Where are you taking it?
To the northern reaches of the Gulf of Maine, where it came from. The water is deep and cold.
Are you sad?
Yes, but doing the right thing is more important than scientific discovery. Thank you for the reminder.
And don't worry. You found this legendary creature. I'm sure you will do other great things, too.
Thank you, my strange young friends.

SURVIVAL TIPS

The simplest way to survive the kraken is to stay away from its **maw**—it can swallow you whole!

* Krakens have never been spotted near a beach.

* The kraken is often attracted to large schools of fish.

* Bubbling water can be a sign that one is near. Calm seas don't bubble.

If you must hunt the kraken, get a submarine. It will be easier to spot under the water.

* Small, quick submarines are best. They're easier to move around.

* Add electricity to the front of the submarine to shock and discourage the kraken from attacking.

* Driving off the kraken may be easier than hunting it down.

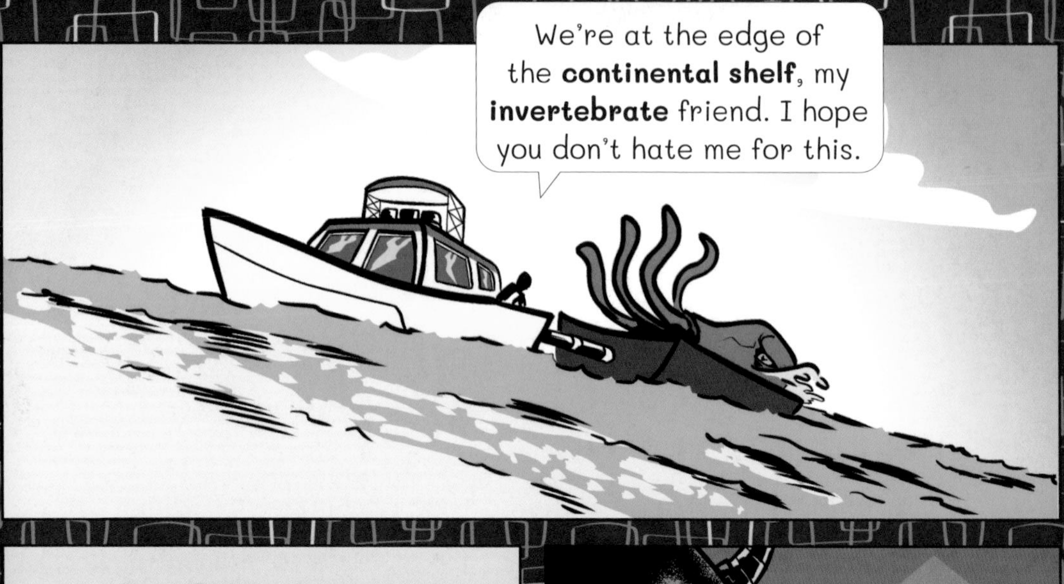
We're at the edge of the **continental shelf**, my **invertebrate** friend. I hope you don't hate me for this.

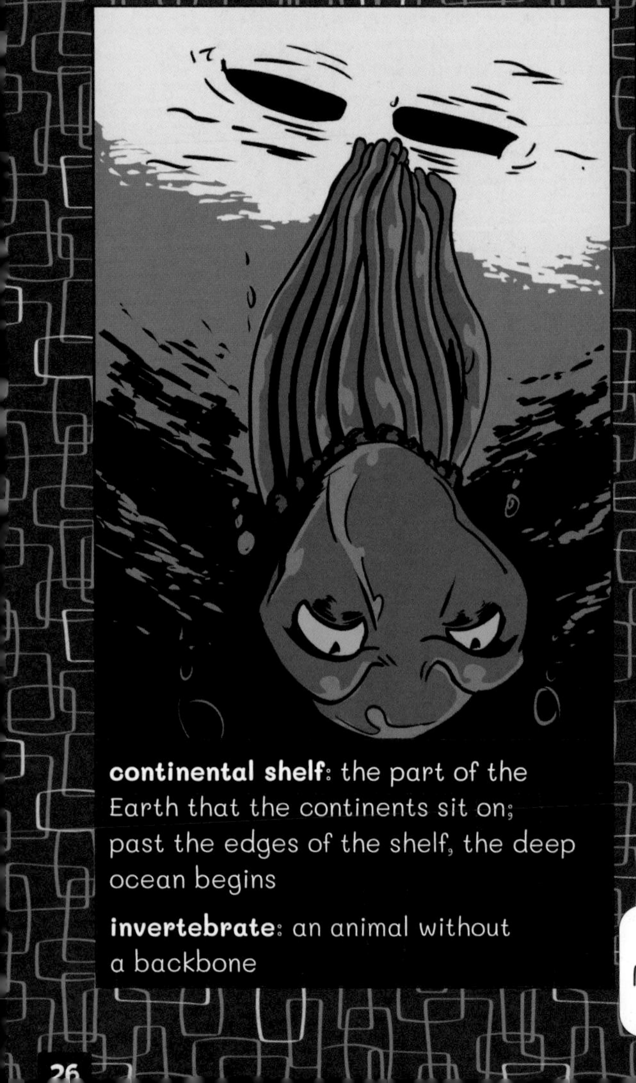

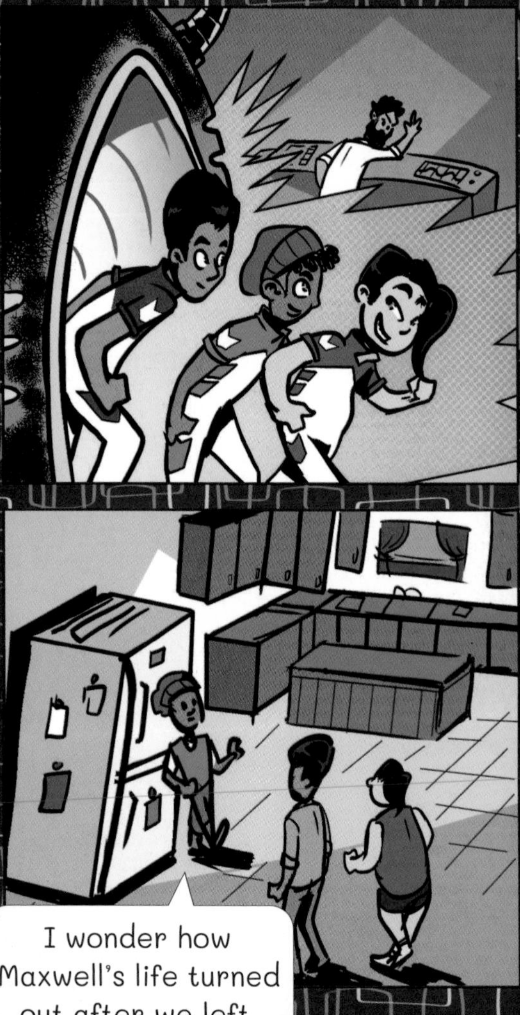
I wonder how Maxwell's life turned out after we left.

continental shelf: the part of the Earth that the continents sit on; past the edges of the shelf, the deep ocean begins

invertebrate: an animal without a backbone

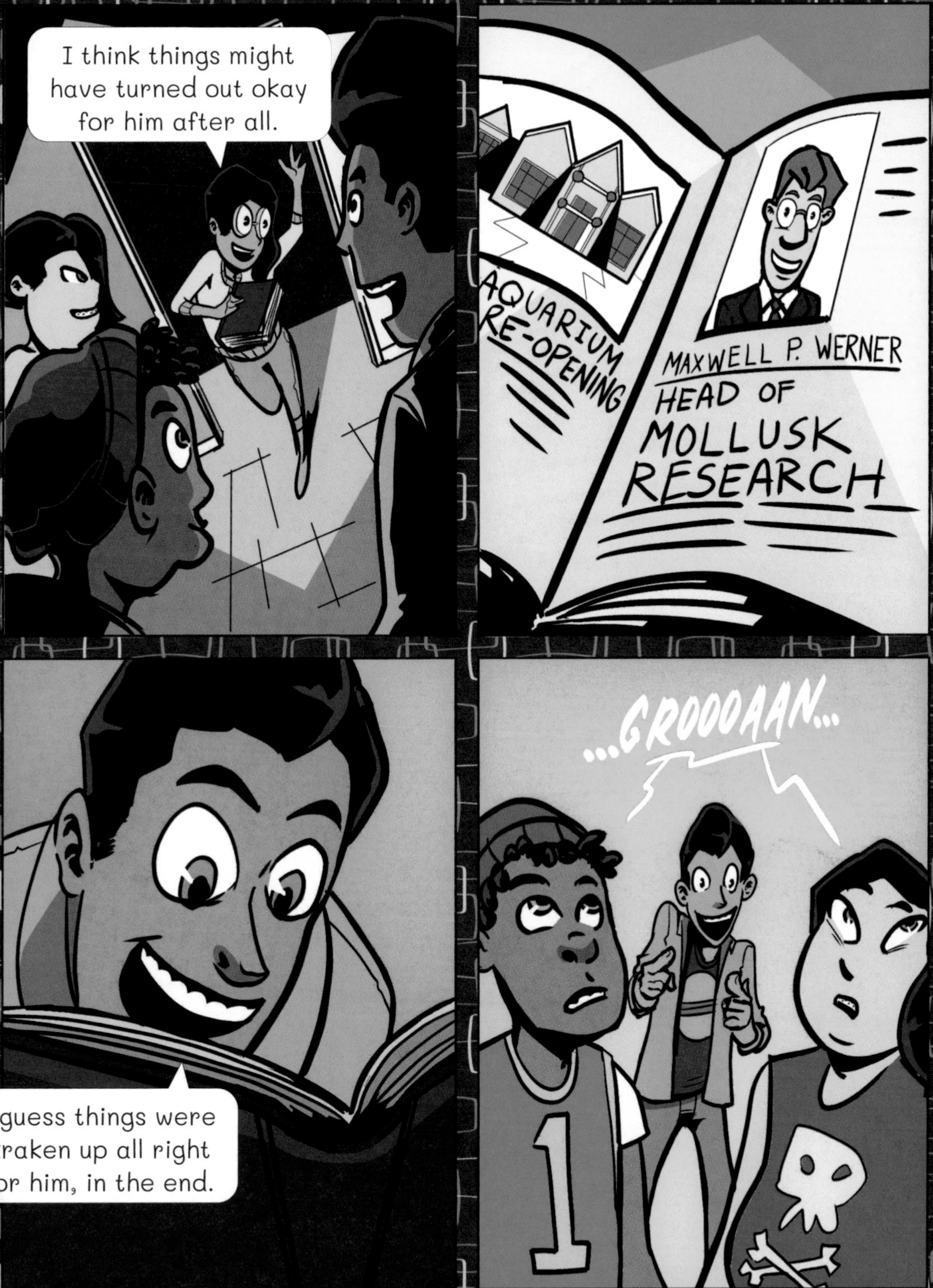
I think things might have turned out okay for him after all.
AQUARIUM RE-OPENING
MAXWELL P. WERNER
HEAD OF MOLLUSK RESEARCH
I guess things were kraken up all right for him, in the end.
...GROOOAAN...

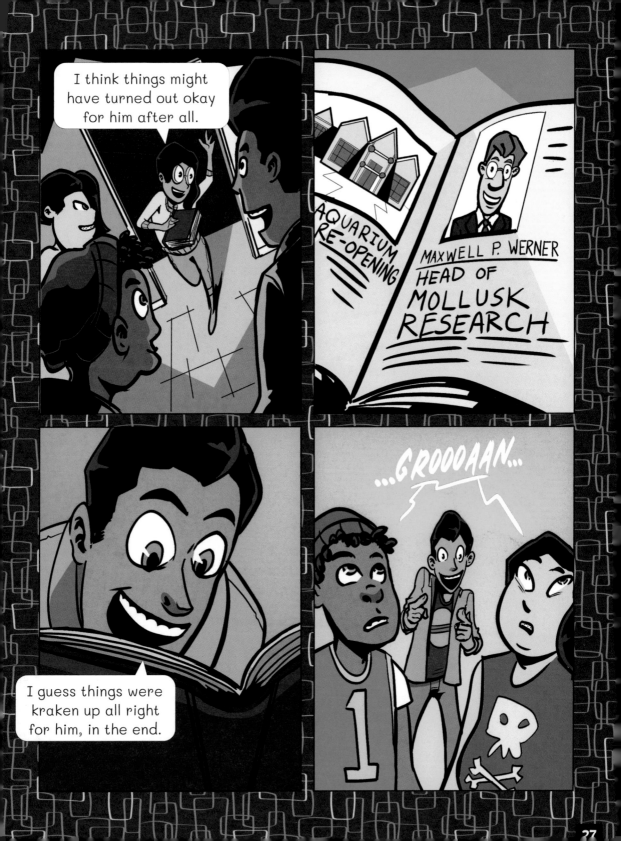

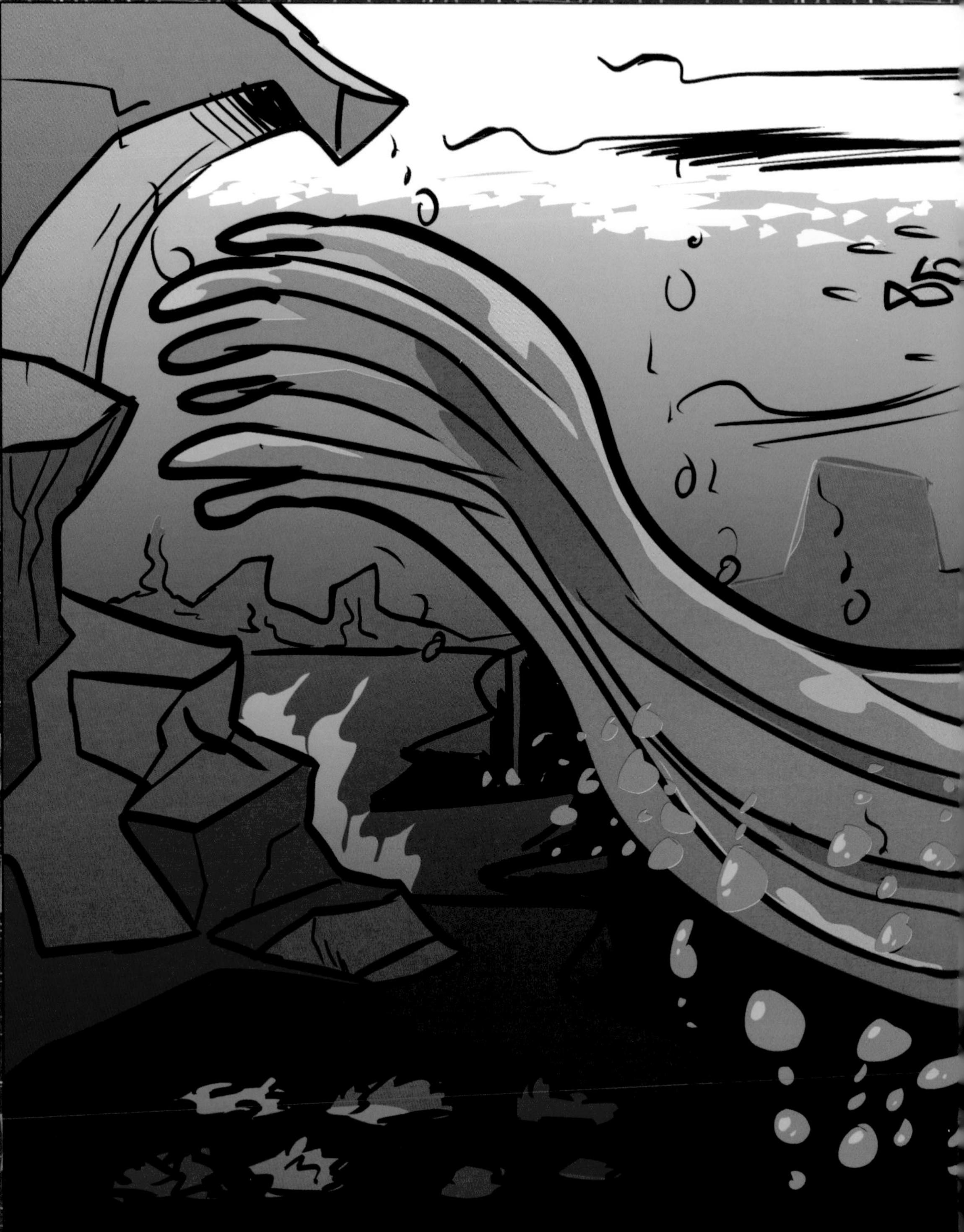

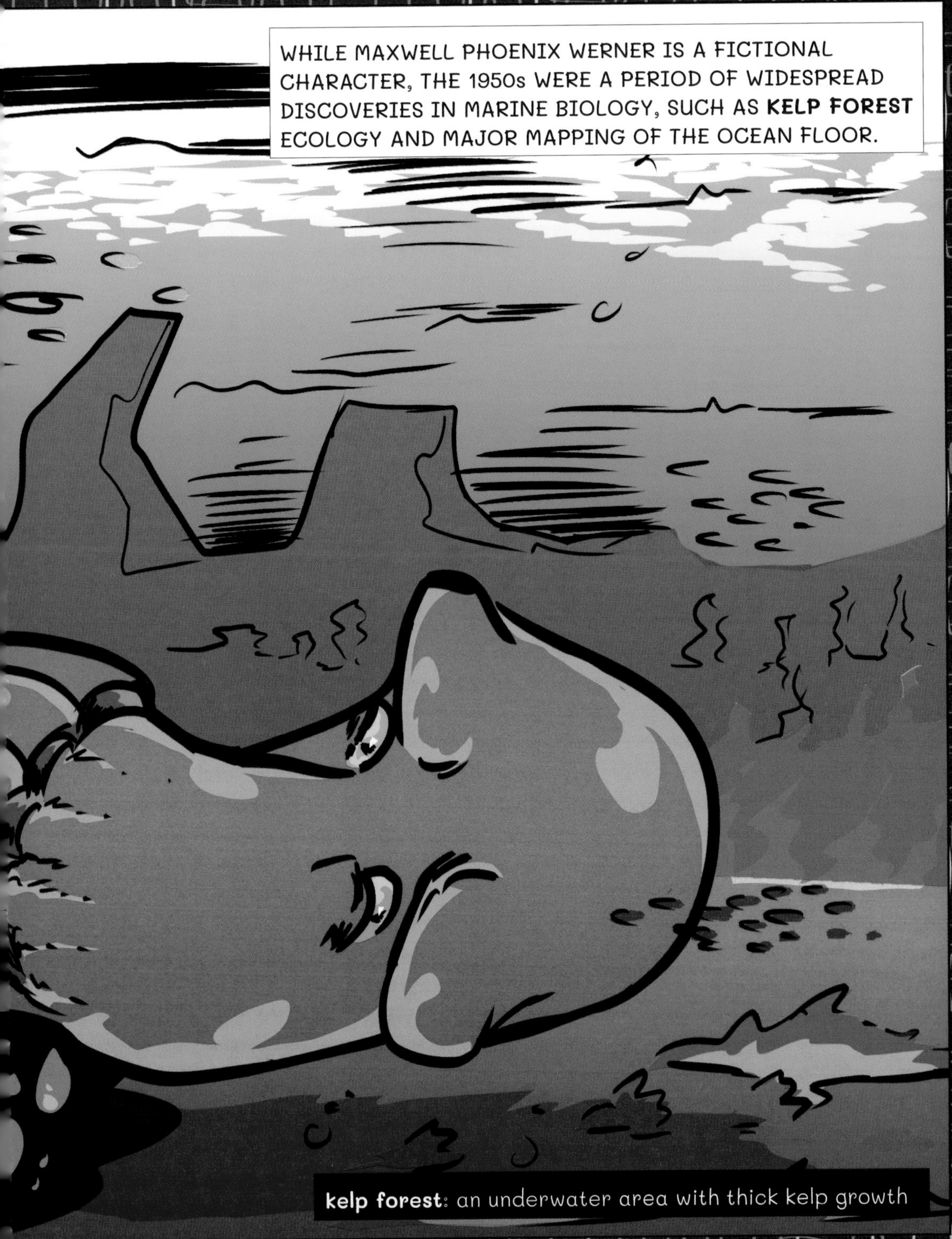
WHILE MAXWELL PHOENIX WERNER IS A FICTIONAL CHARACTER, THE 1950s WERE A PERIOD OF WIDESPREAD DISCOVERIES IN MARINE BIOLOGY, SUCH AS **KELP FOREST** ECOLOGY AND MAJOR MAPPING OF THE OCEAN FLOOR.

kelp forest: an underwater area with thick kelp growth

WRITE A SHORT STORY

Even though Dr. Werner was a scientist and worked with amazing sea creatures, his hobby was baseball. Use your creativity and write a short story that centers around one of your hobbies.

Remember:

* A hobby is something you love to do in your spare time.

* It doesn't matter if you are the best at your hobby. It should be an activity that brings you joy.

* What do you love about your hobby? What makes it challenging?

When creating a story, a good first step is to start with an outline. An outline can answer these questions:

* Where and when does your story take place? This is called the setting.

* How many characters are in your story? What do they look like?

* What challenge will your characters overcome?

Share your story with friends and family. Ask them to share about their own hobbies.

LEARN MORE

BOOKS

Daniele, Kristina Brooke. *Civil Rights, Then & Now: a Timeline of the Fight for Equality in America.* Woodstock, IL: Wendybird Press, 2018.

Hestermann, Josh, and Bethanie Hestermann. *Marine Science for Kids: Exploring and Protecting Our Watery World: Includes Cool Careers and 21 Activities.* Chicago, IL: Chicago Review Press, 2017.

Panchyk, Richard. *Boston History for Kids: from Red Coats to Red Sox with 21 Activities.* Chicago, IL: Chicago Review Press, 2018.

WEBSITES

American Museum of Natural History——Marine Biology: The Living Oceans
https://www.amnh.org/explore/ology/marine-biology

Ducksters——African-American Civil Rights Movement
https:www.ducksters.com/history/civil_rights/african-american_civil_rights_movement.php

THE MONSTER HUNTER TEAM

JORGE
TÍO HECTOR'S NEPHEW, JORGE, LOVES MUSIC. AT 16 HE IS ONE OF THE OLDEST MONSTER HUNTERS AND LEADER OF THE GROUP.

MARCUS
MARCUS IS 14 AND IS WISE BEYOND HIS YEARS. HE IS A PROBLEM SOLVER, OFTEN GETTING THE GROUP OUT OF STICKY SITUATIONS.

FIONA
FIONA IS FIERCE AND PROTECTIVE. AT 16 SHE IS A ROLLER DERBY CHAMPION AND IS ONE OF JORGE'S CLOSEST FRIENDS.

ELENA
ELENA IS JORGE'S LITTLE SISTER AND TÍO HECTOR'S NIECE. AT 14, SHE IS THE HEART AND SOUL OF THE GROUP. ELENA IS KIND, THOUGHTFUL, AND SINCERE.

AMY
AMY IS 15. SHE LOVES BOOKS AND HISTORY. AMY AND ELENA SPEND ALMOST EVERY WEEKEND TOGETHER. THEY ARE ATTACHED AT THE HIP.

TÍO HECTOR
JORGE AND ELENA'S TÍO IS THE MASTERMIND BEHIND THE MONSTER HUNTERS. HIS TIME TRAVEL MACHINE MAKES IT ALL POSSIBLE.

GLOSSARY

arthropods (ARTH-ruh-pahdz) invertebrate animals with a hard shell, like insects, crabs, and spiders

cephalopods (SEH-fuh-luh-pahdz) a group of sea animals with tentacles, like octopus and squid

civil rights (SIH-vul RAITS) the rights for people to have freedom and equality

conformist (kuhn-FOR-mist) accepting of social norms and the established culture

continental shelf (KAHN-tih-nen-tul SHELF) the part of the Earth that the continents sit on; past the edges of the shelf, the deep ocean begins

feminism (FEH-mih-nih-zum) to sift through the ocean with a net

invertebrate (in-VUR-tuh-bret) an animal without a backbone

kelp forest (KEHLP FOR-ist) underwater areas with thick kelp growth

maw (MAH) the jaws and throat of a fearsome animal

ocean floor (OH-shin FLOR) the bottom of the sea

page (PAYJ) to call someone over an intercom system

rationed (RA-shend) when each person is allowed only a certain amount of something

segregation (seh-greh-GAY-shun) the separation of people based on the color of their skin

tentacles (TEN-tuh-kulz) thin, flexible limbs

tío (TEE-oh) "uncle" in Spanish

trawling (TRAH-ling) sifting through the ocean with a net

INDEX